THE AMERICAN COMMON LAW
THE CUSTOMARY LAW OF THE AMERICAN NATION

HANDED DOWN THROUGH THE AGES
CODIFIED BY
MARCUS HATFIELD
FOR THE BENEFIT OF ALL TRUE AMERICANS EVERYWHERE
@2015

Introduction

What is common law?

Common law is that portion of the law that exists outside of statutory law, or legislation. It is often unwritten. It includes the precedents of the courts, but it also includes that portion of the law that is established by custom. Customary law makes up most of the unwritten portion of the common law. Customary law or traditional law is that portion of the law that is passed down by more or less universal agreement, tradition, and precedent of usage. Some of it is based upon the rulings of the courts, and some of it is far more ancient than any citation that a lawyer could find.

What is the purpose of the American Common Law?

The purpose of the American Common Law is to provide a codification of the common law that has traditionally governed the American people. As of 2015, the American people are being governed by the Constitution of 1789, under the states and the federal government. This present system of government could become undesirable or impractical. For example, a tyrannical government could seize control of the federal system, and make it unsuitable for the government of the American people. Some would argue that has already taken place. Alternately, federal and state authority could break down for a number of other reasons, such as economic collapse, natural disaster, man-made disaster, or political turmoil. In such a case, the American Nation might need to resume governing itself under customary law. A very brief codification of the essentials of American customary law is essential for carrying out the traditional American form of government in the absence of taxes, specialized legal experts, professional police, or trained judges. The American people have always been a self-governing people, and this codification makes it possible for that self-government to continue in the absence of legislatively constructed authority.

The purpose of the American Common Law is contained in the questions, "Could American law and justice survive in a TEOTWAWKI situation? Could American law be carried out by a resistance movement to tyranny? An underground government without prisons, professional police, or lawyers?" The answer, I believe, is, "Yes." This is the constitution for your traditional American legal system, divorced from specialization. It is rough, but it is just. And it provides continuity of American law and justice for the American Nation in the worst of times.

What is the American Nation?

The American Nation is a group of Celtic and Anglo-Saxon people who settled in British North America, bringing their uniquely libertarian Anglo-Saxon common law with them. The Angles and Saxons had earlier brought their common law to Britain, when they immigrated there some thousand years before and conquered, assimilated, or displaced the Celtic British tribes who lived there before them. In 1789, the United States government was created as a government for the American Nation, but the two are distinct. Membership in the American Nation is distinct from United States citizenship. In the 1860's, the African slaves of the American Nation were incorporated into the American Nation as full members, while they were also given United States citizenship. Over the years, many other immigrants were assimilated into the American Nation (not all immigrants have assimilated). However, the American Nation remains the descendants of Anglo-Saxon people who immigrated to British North America, no less than the Sioux people remain the descendants of Asian people who immigrated earlier to North America. The American Nation is European in culture, is of the Christian religion, and this booklet contains our traditional law. Anyone of any background may assimilate into the American Nation, but only those of American culture and religion are members. The traditional part of our law and culture can be practiced without the specialized apparatus of the US government, as it was practiced in the past, by means of this booklet.

How does this booklet do this?

By laying out the basic principles of the common law county, the most basic institution of American national government, this codification of American customary law makes possible the continuity of American National government even after the demise of the federal government of the United States.

What is the authority of this law?

This law rests on the authority of precedent. It is the law as received by us from our forebears. As such, it may not be up to date with the latest legal precedents or legislation, neither does it need to be. This law rests in the authority of the American common law, passed down to us by our forefathers. It underlies all law, at all times, and by virtue of its traditional power binds all Americans. It is possible to put into effect at any time and place, does not cost much of any money, and requires only a properly educated people to put into practice.

What education is necessary?

It is necessary only that the American people who put it into practice know, understand, and substantially agree with the contents of this little booklet. If there are disagreements with the traditional law, there are a number of safeguards in the law to prevent it from becoming a tyrannical law. The traditional law includes jury nullification. If any law becomes so out of date as to be detestable to the people, the juries may disregard it.

What people might practice it?

This is written for the benefit of the American people, but any people who desire to may adopt it and use it. They will have success in proportion to their virtue and their education. If the people have the strength to reach for it, this book tells in 21 pages how they may live free in a free county.

Is the idea of a free county that stands alone ridiculous?

Many free cities or microstates have risen throughout history. Modern examples include Monaco, Liechtenstein, and Luxembourg. These microstates boast among the highest income and personal freedom of all states. For over four hundred years, who would rather have lived in China than in Hong Kong?

The most important functions of American law are all performed by the county. No matter where Americans have traveled or settled, the county functions have served as the foundation for all government. The needs of an urban county are different than the needs of a rural county, but each has the resources to meet its needs. The needs of the common law county are few indeed, as the government is stripped down to its most necessary functions. There is no reason to believe that an alliance of such counties wouldn't be a power to be reckoned with.

The Common Law County

Section 1: Instituting American Common Law

Part A: American Common Law may be instituted in any county presently or formerly part of the United States by a majority vote in a popular election in that county. Once adopted, it cannot be repealed.

Part B: The election must be announced at least thirty days in advance by at least one of the two following methods:

    i.   By publishing at least twice in the major newspaper of the county.
    ii.   By posting handbills in the major stores and commercial centers of the county.

No part of the county should be neglected. The notices must specify the place and the time of the election, as well as the fact that the election shall be for the purpose of implementing the American Common Law. Any male citizen of the American Nation may vote in the election.

Part C: The election can be held under the laws of the United States, or any state thereof, or under the supervision of a private organization. If it is held under the laws of a state or the United States, a resolution that would be otherwise legally non-binding or advisory shall be considered binding for the purposes of this election.

Part D: If the election is successful, the county shall be considered an American Common Law County. It is a free county, not subject to any state or federal law, the treaty, or the Constitution of 1789, and is completely self-governing under the American Common Law. If the election is successful, this fact shall be promulgated throughout the county by like means to Part B.

Section 2: Offices in the American Common Law County

Part A: The offices in the common law county shall be as follows:

    i. Sheriff at Common Law, or Sheriff. The county Sheriff shall be the chief law enforcement officer of the county. He shall have the responsibility to keep the peace, to serve warrants, complaints, and subpoenas, and to safeguard prisoners prior to trial. When the grand jury is summoned, he will give them their charge, and return both no bills and indictments to the county judge. If he is the subject of the investigation, the county judge shall do his duty. The Sheriff shall examine the county records of the counties money annually. He can summon as many able bodied men of the county as necessary to serve as deputies to assist him in carrying out his responsibilities on a temporary basis. He shall carry out the sentences of the court, including fining, whipping, and hanging.

    ii. County Justice at Common Law, or County Judge. The county judge shall preside at all trials under the American Common Law, shall hear complaints, both civil and criminal, and shall issue orders, judgments, warrants, and subpoenas as necessary to carry out the law. He shall record the details of all land sales in the appropriate county records, and maintain the money of the county. In the event of riot, insurrection, or invasion he may call out the militia of the county. In the event of necessity, he may hire clerks to carry out such non-judicial duties as he sees fit if the money is available.

    iii. Colonel of County Militia. The Colonel of County Militia will command the able bodied armed men of the county. He shall conduct a muster, or gathering, each year at which every man must attend bearing a firearm and ammunition, provided he is not conscientiously opposed to warfare. The Colonel of County Militia will command the militia of the county in case of war, invasion, riot, or insurrection. He will provide for the election of inferior officers should the militia go into service for an extended period of time. During peacetime, the Colonel shall encourage the training of the men of the county in warfare and marksmanship.

Part B: Elections

i. Elections shall thereafter be held at a convenient public place, every four years.
ii. Elections shall be announced 30 days prior to the election.
iii. Elections shall not be held by secret ballot. In order to prevent fraud, each vote will be read out loud and recorded in a public manner.
iv. In the event of the death of an office holder, a special election to fill the vacancy shall be announced immediately, and election shall be held 30 days subsequent to fill that office only.
v. Any male member of the American Nation shall be eligible to vote provided he speaks English, has registered to vote at least 30 days prior to the election, and has paid his annual capitation if due.
vi. Citizenship in the American Nation shall be as follows:
   1. Descendants of those Anglo-Saxon and other Germanic and Celtic people who settled North America in the 18th century.
   2. Descendants of their African servants, who obtained citizenship under the 13th Amendment.

3. Descendants of subsequent immigrants to North America, provided at least one of their grandfathers were citizens or registered voters of the United States or members of the American Nation.
4. Descendants of those who obtained citizenship in the United States under the Snyder Act.

Part C. Taxes

i. Every government must tax. The Common Law County is limited to a capitation, payable annually by every male resident of the county who is registered to vote. The county judge, sheriff, and colonel of militia shall meet annually to set the tax rate, if any. Those who do not pay, may not vote. Additionally, the county may sue to collect taxes owed and if judgment is rendered, may punish non-payment as contempt of court. In times of famine and disruption, it is expected that the county shall maintain itself sometimes without taxes.

Section 3: Customary Criminal Offenses

A: Felonies. There are 13 Customary Felonies.
i. Murder. Murder is the unlawful killing of another person without legal justification, with premeditation.
    a. Persons who kill another in self-defense or defense of another are not guilty of murder.
    b. Persons who kill another person in a fight to which all parties consented are not guilty of murder.
    c. Persons who kill another person by accident are not guilty of murder.
    d. Persons who kill another person in the heat of the moment, through extreme provocation are not guilty of murder, particularly if the killing was provoked by the commission of adultery wherein the person killed was guilty of adultery against the person who killed him.
    e. Persons who are defending their health from great bodily harm or their property or that of another may kill another person without committing murder.
    f. Persons who are attempting to capture a fleeing felon who cannot be captured by other means who kill the felon are not guilty of murder.
    g. During honorable service in the militia during warfare, insurrection, riot, or other deadly confrontation persons may kill without committing murder, whether or not in self-defense.
ii. Burglary. Burglary is the entry of a home or other building for the sole purpose of committing a theft.

iii. Robbery. Robbery is committing a theft by force or the threat of the use of force.
iv. Arson. Arson is the destruction of property by means of fire.
v. Kidnapping. To unlawfully confine, steal, and imprison a man or woman by force, or to steal a child from its parents.
vi. Rape. For any man to unlawfully use force or threat of harm to engage in sexual intercourse with any woman who is not his wife.
vii. Grand Theft. To unlawfully and permanently obtain the use or possession of any property of a value more than an ounce of gold, or to permanently deprive any person of such property by destroying it, or to poison a well or stream of water, or the air in a certain area not his own property, and make it unfit for use.
viii. Child Molestation. For a person who is above the age of puberty to engage in sexual intercourse or sodomy with a child who has not yet reached puberty is child molestation.
ix. Sodomy. Sodomy is fellatio, cunnilingus, or anal intercourse between two persons of the same sex, or any of these three acts between two persons of opposite sexes when one of them has reached puberty and the other has not yet reached puberty, OR any of these acts incestuously carried out between natural parent and child or between adult siblings.
x. Perjury. A person commits perjury who knowingly makes a false statement under oath or affirmation if that statement is material to the outcome of a trial. Likewise a person who induces another to do the same commits perjury.

xi. Bribery. Offering, giving, receiving, or soliciting of any item of value to influence the actions of an official or other person in charge of a public or legal duty.

xii. Witchcraft. To attempt to curse or otherwise do harm to another person through magic, shamanism, folk practices, calling on elementals and spirits or the devil, or veneration of ancient pagan deities, or offering for sale deadly poisons for the purpose of killing another person, or for harming them, or to do or offer to do any act or administer any poison causing abortion of a pregnancy, whether or not such activities actually case a person harm.

xiii. Heinous battery. To unlawfully and without justification:
   A. burn any person with fire or acid or harm with poison,
   B. to cut off a limb,
   C. or put out an eye or otherwise blind any person,
   D. to damage their mental function or powers,
   E. to render them impotent or infertile,
   F. or to knock out any person's tooth or teeth.

   It is a justification and defense that such injury occurred during defense of life, health, or property against a criminal act, or if the circumstances would be a valid defense against a charge of murder. Patria potestas is not a defense to heinous battery.

B. Misdemeanors. There are five misdemeanors.

i. Breach of the Peace. A person commits breach of the peace if he:

a. Interferes with or disrupts a funeral service, wedding, or worship service.

b. Blocks a road or highway with the intent of disrupting other's ability to use it.

c. Discharges or brandishes a firearm in an alarming or frightening way.

d. Displays his genitals, buttocks, or the breasts of a female in public in a careless way without consideration of who is present,

e. Makes a false alarm of a fire, crime, accident, or injury or summons a grand jury without cause.

f. Peeps into a restroom, changing area, or other place where people are accustomed to change clothing or disrobe for purposes of sexual gratification or to embarrass the other persons.

g. Interferes with an election.

h. Conducts themselves in such a reckless way as to place reasonable persons in fear of an accident.

ii. Battery. A person commits battery by striking or otherwise making provoking or injurious contact with another person, or by throwing or shooting an object or substance at them which strikes them, or by spitting on them. Self defense or participation in a fight agreed to by all parties is a defense. Reasonable corporal punishment exercised through patria potestas by a father, mother, or husband and not resulting in permanent injury or impairment is not battery.

iii. Assault. A person commits assault by undertaking any action which would place a reasonable person in fear of receiving a battery.

iv.	Theft. Depriving or attempting to deprive a person permanently of the use of property of a value less than an ounce of gold by taking it or by destroying it in an unlawful manner is theft.
v.	Adultery. A person commits adultery by having sexual intercourse with a married person not his wife or husband.

Section 4: Criminal Process

A. No criminal prosecution for any felony shall begin without an indictment. No person charged with a felony may be imprisoned for more than 24 hours without an indictment by the grand jury. No one can be imprisoned more than 24 hours for a misdemeanor without seeing a judge to establish probable cause.
B. A grand jury may be summoned by any citizen of the American Nation by making a written complaint of the commission of a felony to the county sheriff, or if the county sheriff is the alleged offender, to the county judge.
C. A grand jury shall consist of 24 adult male citizens of the American Nation who reside in the county. They shall be selected by the Sheriff (or County Judge if the Sheriff is accused) and shall serve a term of one year.
D. The grand jury shall be summoned as provided by law, shall appoint a foreman, and then shall conduct an investigation of the crime. The grand jury may investigate any crimes that are complained of to them in writing, or any other crimes that they become aware of by other means. If the grand jury shall vote by majority, that probable cause exists to believe the crime was committed, they shall return a true bill of indictment. If no probable cause exists, they shall return a no bill.
E. If a true bill is returned, the county judge shall issue a warrant for the arrest of the accused. No warrants for arrest or search warrants shall issue except upon probably cause. No searches shall be undertaken, except in emergency situations, without a warrant. Even in emergency situations probable cause must exist, or the evidence shall be inadmissible.
F. Reasonable bail should be set unless there is a strong likelihood of flight.
G. An arrestee shall be brought as soon as possible before the judge, and trial shall be held within 30 days, unless good

cause exists to delay the trial such as unavailability of witnesses or evidence.
H. All trials should be held within thirty days, unless the delay is the fault of the accused. Persons not brought to trial within thirty days of apprehension shall have charges dismissed with prejudice.
I. No husband shall testify against his wife, neither shall wife testify against husband. Each person may claim only one wife or husband. A marriage shall exist for this purpose where two persons of the opposite sex, not closer related by blood or marriage than a second cousin, announce themselves publicly as wife or husband, and have a history of cohabitation.
J. No one shall be subject to torture, neither shall the accused be compelled to testify against himself. The accused shall have the right to summon witnesses, and to review all evidence prior to the trial. Charges shall not be changed or amended during the trial. The prosecution must bring the case as originally charged, except for the case of perjury.
K. The jury shall be charged in the following manner by the county judge:

"Members of the jury: You shall hear all the evidence and argument with an open mind, disregarding your affections and prejudices. You may find the accused innocent for any reason, or for no reason at all, but if you find him guilty it must be for no other reason than you believe him to be guilty beyond a reasonable doubt. The right of jury nullification is absolute."

L. If the accused is found to be innocent, he will go free and never be troubled again on this account. There must be no double jeopardy.
M. If the accused is found guilty, he will be given seven days to present an appeal to the county judge. Then punishment shall be carried out swiftly.

N. Punishments for felonies are decided by the jury. Punishments for misdemeanors are decided by the judge.
O. The punishment for felonies are as follows:
   a. On first offense the convict is to be fined the value of one to ten ounces of gold. Murderers, rapists, heinous batterers, and child molesters shall be flogged with up to 39 lashes.
   b. On second conviction for the same felony crime, the convict is to be flogged with no more than 39 lashes. On the second conviction for rape, sodomy, or child molestation a male convict shall have his genitals severed with a sharp hatchet. On second conviction, all convicts of rape, sodomy, and child molestation shall have their cheeks branded with a hot iron with the letter M to warn others.
   c. On third offense for the same crime, the convict is to be hung by the neck until he is dead. If the rope breaks or the hanging is otherwise thwarted by circumstance, the convict shall go free.
P. The punishment for misdemeanors is to be fining the value of one to ten ounces of silver on first offense. At the discretion of the judge, the misdemeanor convict can be flogged with one to ten lashes in addition to fine for subsequent misdemeanor convictions.
Q. No doctor or other medical person shall have any part in castration, branding, or hanging, but may administer care following castration or branding. Branding, castration, or flogging shall be the responsibility of the Sheriff or his deputy. The bill for any medical care shall go to the convict, not the county.
R. Criminal trials will be conducted under the rules laid out in the section on civil process.

Section 5: Civil Process

Part A: Civil Complaints

1. All civil complaints will be presented to the county judge in writing.
2. A copy shall be delivered to the other party by the county sheriff.
3. Where the matter involves less than ten ounces of silver in controversy, each party shall make his case orally before the county judge—and shall present such witnesses and evidence as he has without the use of the subpoena power. All pleadings shall state the value of property at stake.
4. Where more than ten ounces of silver is at stake, the parties may compel witnesses and the production of evidence by subpoena.
5. Cases over ten ounces silver worth may be tried by jury on motion of either party. Otherwise, they are tried by judge only.
6. The judge shall make his ruling in writing, and it shall contain a summary of the facts and the basis of the decision as well as the judgment.
7. Each party has 7 days to make an appeal to the county judge.
8. After 7 days, the judgment shall be swiftly obeyed. The judge has the power to punish contempt with one to three ounces of silver fine, or in extreme cases with one to three strokes of the lash. Persons who are unable or who refuse to pay fines and judgments are subject to having their labor for a definite term sold at public auction to pay the fine or judgment.
9. The county shall not involve itself in marriages or divorces, other than for the purpose of the privilege of testimony. These are private or religious matters.
10. Only the biological or adoptive mother or father of a child may sue for sole custody. The court shall presume that the best interests of the child are to reside with his

biological father, absent evidence that the father is a felon under the American Common Law. Evidence of felon status shall consist only of a record of conviction under the courts of the American Common Law, and shall rebut the presumption of paternal superiority. The rights of a child's natural fit parents shall pre-empt all other claims of custody of a child. Parents shall have the sole right to provide and judge the education of children. There shall be no money awarded for child support.
11. All pleadings shall be written in the English language.
12. In all matters before the court, the county judge shall make his rulings based on law and equity.
13. Jurors will be chosen by the county judge, and must be honest men without a stake in the matter. In both criminal and civil cases there shall be 12 jurors. Jurors must find unanimously. If a jury fails to reach a verdict, in both civil and criminal cases double jeopardy attaches, and no further proceedings may be brought in the matter.
14. No one may charge money to represent another in court under penalty of contempt.
15. Anyone may bring a friend to represent them, provided they do not charge money for the representation.
16. No hearsay shall be allowed, except for documentary exceptions. Hearsay is testimony of things said out of court, and presented as evidence of the truth of the matter asserted. Except for the documentary exception, all declarations must be made in court, in front of the judge, and subject to cross examination.
17. The county shall not hear petitions seeking to have children removed from their parents without evidence of a felony criminal conviction in the courts of the American Common Law.
18. Evidence that is irrelevant may not be admitted.
19. In both civil and criminal matters, there is no identity shield. The accused right to face his accuser and to have a public trial are paramount.
20. All trials must be public.

21. Members of the clergy are privileged from revealing what is disclosed to them by persons seeking their counsel.
22. Reporters are privileged from revealing sources, except for in cases involving slander and libel.
23. The following are recognized torts:
    a. Trespass to land. Anyone who enters another's land without permission and especially where a sign is posted may be required to pay reasonable damages for trespass to land.
    b. Assault. A person who is the victim of actions that would place a reasonable person in fear of receiving a battery may sue for assault and recover damages.
    c. Battery. A person who is the victim of unlawful physical provoking or injurious contact, by whatever means, which is made by reckless or intentional conduct is liable for damages for battery.
    d. Mayhem. Mayhem is defined as any medical treatment rendered without the consent of the person treated, or in the case of a minor, the consent of the father or mother. If the person is found unconscious and cannot consent to treatment, it is a defense to mayhem. A person who commits mayhem is liable for damages.
    e. False imprisonment. A person who without lawful justification confines another is liable for damages for false imprisonment. Shopkeepers may confine suspected thieves reasonably, as may other citizens who reasonably suspect a crime, provided they summon the Sheriff in a reasonable time.
    f. Trespass to Chattels. A person who, without lawful justification, holds another person's property, wife, or children is liable for damages for trespass to chattels.
    g. Libel and Slander. A person who makes a spoken statement that was false, caused harm, and was made without adequate research into the truthfulness of

the statement is liable for slander. If the statement is printed, the person is liable for libel.
    h. Seduction. A person who seduces a young woman with false promises of marriage is liable for damages for seduction.
    i. Breach of contract. A person commits breach of contract when he fails to perform any act that he is required to do or performs any act he is prohibited from doing under the terms of any written contract, notarized or otherwise attested to, and is liable for damages.
    j. No other torts are recognized than this list.
24. All trials must be held within 30 days of the service of the complaint, and not less than seven days after service of the complaint.
25. Trials are not to be televised or video recorded, upon penalty of contempt. They can be audio recorded if it is possible.
26. Respondents who are entirely justified by the court are entitled to damages for lost time to be paid by the complainant. In other words, loser pays. Loser paid damages are assessed by the court following the jury verdict.
27. In all trials, a strict colorblindness must be practiced by judge and jury, and while private association and private property are absolute rights, government must be free of racial animus and prejudice. Juries will be charged in civil proceedings as follows: "You jurors will make your ruling on the basis of the law and evidence before you, and will lay aside your affections and prejudices so as to return an equitable verdict. If you believe one party to be at least 70% at fault in the matter, and are convinced that the evidence is clear and convincing, you must return a verdict in favor of the aggrieved party. Otherwise, you must not return any verdict."

28. All members of the American Nation shall have the right to make contracts freely, and to have those contracts enforced in the Common Law Courts.

Section 6: Confederation and the State

A. County is Basic Unit, Sovereign

1. This county is a free and sovereign government.
2. This county is free to ally itself with other counties that practice the American Common Law form of government.
3. In the event that counties ally themselves together, an American Common Law State can be formed.
4. Each county will serve as the legislative district for a unicameral House of Representatives.
5. That House of Representatives will choose a governor.
6. Taxes shall be apportioned equally among the counties, by population.
7. The state shall respect each county's sovereignty.
8. The governor shall lead the state in the event of war, otherwise he shall preside over the legislature.
9. No law shall interfere with or alter the operation of the American Common Law.
10. Each county shall have the right to withdraw from its state, and to join another state without fear of compulsion.
11. The state's representatives shall draw up a state constitution on traditional and common law principles.

Comments on Male Privilege in the Common Law

The following explanations are given for the choice of certain traditional laws and practices. Men alone are able to vote and serve as jurors and officeholders under this traditional law. The reason this is so, is because there are only 12 men on a jury and only 24 on a grand jury. A numerous family could be called to serve, and if the wives were also permitted to serve it would result in undue influence being given to a single family and by extension to the head of that family. If a man and his wife both served, it would be as though he had two votes instead of one. Similarly, in some circumstances, very small numbers of votes will decide elections. Since giving the women the vote in the United States, women have returned the victory of every socialist and every progressive candidate in the history of the United States. It is not intended that this error should be perpetuated in the American Common Law, and American and Anglo-Saxon law provide ample precedent for limiting the vote to men only. The presumption in favor of a man over a woman in child custody is based in Roman and American legal precedent, as well as in the scientific finding that the single best indicator of success for children is residence with their biological father. This assumption is rebuttable if a felony conviction under the American Common Law exists. Fines and values are given in ounces of gold or silver, because other currency is subject to changes in relative value. Fines can be paid in whatever form is customary, but will be assessed according the present value in gold or silver.

www.ingramcontent.com/pod-product-compliance
Lightning Source LLC
Chambersburg PA
CBHW021000180526
45163CB00006B/2436